Summary of

The New Jim Crow
Michelle Alexander

Conversation Starters

By BookHabits

Please Note: This is an unofficial conversation starters guide. If you have not yet read the original work or would like to read it again, get the book here.

We hope you enjoy this complementary guide from BookHabits.
Our mission is to aid readers and reading groups with quality, thought provoking material to in the discovery and discussions on some of today's favorite books.

Tips for Using BookHabits Conversation Starters

EVERY GOOD BOOK CONTAINS A WORLD FAI
DEEPER THAN the surface of its pages. Th
characters and their world come alive through th
words on the pages, yet the characters and its worl
still live on. Questions herein are designed to bring
us beneath the surface of the page and invite us int
the world that lives on. These questions can be used
to:

- Foster a deeper understanding of the book
- Promote an atmosphere of discussion fo groups
- Assist in the study of the book, eithe individually or corporately
- Explore unseen realms of the book as neve seen before

About Us:

THROUGH YEARS OF EXPERIENCE AND FIELL
EXPERTISE, from newspaper featured book clubs to
local library chapters, *BookHabits* can bring you
book discussion to life. Host your book party as we
discuss some of today's most widely read books.

Table of Contents

Introducing *The New Jim Crow*

*T*he New Jim Crow* asserts that mass incarceration in the US is the new form of discrimination against African Americans. By legalizing harsh drug laws that put blacks in jail, they are prevented from fully taking advantage of their rights. It keeps them from participating in economic, political and social privileges as American citizens and relegates them to society's margins. In this way, the incarcerated and formerly incarcerated are much like in the same condition as heir forefathers who were discriminated in the late 19th and early 20th centuries through Jim Crow laws.

Before she came to write the book, Michelle Alexander thought that a full-scale discrimination against blacks is a story of the past. Today, African Americans' lives have progressed since slavery days. Her work with the American Civil Liberties Union (ACLU) however opened her eyes to the reality which she now reveals in her book. Chapter One orients the reader on the history of how racism started in America, covering landmark events and developments including Jim Crow laws that relegated blacks into inferior beings, the Reconstruction, and the Civil Rights Movement. A backlash resulted from the Civil Rights Movement, and consequently led to President Ronald Reagan's sensationalized campaign against drugs, legalizing harsh punishment for offenders which targeted many blacks. President Bill Clinton's policies further legalized unfair treatment for blacks. The New Jim Crow is a result of these developments over the years. Chapter Two explains how mass incarceration is similar to a caste system. Beliefs and stereotypes that reinforce this caste system are discussed. Chapter Three reveals how racism operates in the criminal justice system, and how the few legal means to redress cannot really be of use to blacks. Chapter Four is an examination of how former inmates face numerous obstacles as they attempt to be reintegrated in society. Chapter Five identifies the similarities and differences between the Jim Crow laws in the past and the system of mass incarceration today. The new Jim Crow is similar to the past one in several instances including the racial segregation of neighborhoods, disenfranchisement, and legalized discrimination. It discusses how many blacks and other citizens choose to ignore the new Jim Crow thus preventing activists from taking real action to stop the ongoing discrimination. Chapter 6 asks the question of why civil rights activists are not protesting against mass incarceration. She criticizes the ineffectiveness of Affirmative Action and makes suggestions on how to start a concerted effort to deal with the real problem of the new Jim Crow.

The book is packed with carefully researched data which show the truth about incarceration. The author uses strong imagery to portray important situations, like persecution in the ghettos and the terror felt in face of police intimidation. The motif of closures and mazes is used to stress the difficulty of using the legal system to get justice for black victims of discrimination. Another motif is the language of denial which is often used by politicians and law officers who claim to be colorblind but don't recognize the racist effects of their actions. The symbols used in the book include the noose, the box, and the character of Rosa Parks. The noose represents violence committed against blacks, the box is a symbol of social stigma done to the formerly ncarcerated, and Rosa Parks symbolizes the fight against discrimination. Alexander points out ronies that give light to the new Jim Crow situation. The support that blacks give to harsh discipline to control inner city crime is used by conservative politicians to further block racial progress. Another rony is that while studies show that white professionals most likely engage in drug use, it is blacks rather than whites who are most often apprehended. The ultimate irony cited in the book s that while this is supposedly the age of colorblindness, there is the real issue of the undercaste system being created by the new Jim Crow apparent in the case of incarcerated blacks.

The New Jim Crow was first published in 2010 and was on *The New York Times* bestseller list for over a year. It won the NAACP Image Award for best nonfiction in 2011. It is considered the secular bible by social activists who cite the book in their consciousness raising activities in schools, colleges, churches, community centers and prisons all over the country. The *New York Review of Books* applauds *The New Jim Crow* for the intelligence of Alexander's ideas, her powerful summary of the situation, and her forceful writing. Book critics have praised Alexander for her "vigorous and persuasive" language, and her ability to make abstract ideas clear.

Discussion Questions

"Get Ready to Enter a New World"

Tip: Begin with questions dealing with broader issues to ensure ample time for quality discussions. Read through all discussion questions before engaging.

~ ~ ~

question 1

While working for the ACLU, Michelle Alexander saw how the criminal justice system was biased against blacks. The system rendered blacks second class citizens. Before Alexander's book, did you think the criminal justice system was being fair to all Americans? Why? Why not?

~ ~ ~

~~~

question 2

The Jim Crow laws rendered blacks inferior to whites by disallowing them political, economic, and social privileges. Why does Alexander think the new Jim Crow is similar to the past one? Are blacks still considered inferior today?

~~~

~~~

question 3

Alexander tells the history of racial relations in America in the first chapter of the book. She discusses slavery in the past and how the fight for black emancipation led to the Civil War, the Reconstruction, the Jim Crow laws, and the Civil Rights Movement. What can you say about the history of fight for racial equality in the US? Do you think African Americans and those who support human rights will keep on fighting for real freedom and equality in the years to come?

~~~

~ ~ ~

question 4

President Ronald Reagan started the War on Drugs in the 1980s. Alexander says the statistics then did not show a drug problem on the rise but Reagan sensationalized it in the media to make it appear real. Why did Reagan declare the War on drugs if there was no escalating drug problem? Who were the first to suffer as a result?

~ ~ ~

question 5

Some of the most severe anti-drug laws were passed during the time of President Bill Clinton. The laws further put stress on black families who were economically disadvantaged. Would you have expected Clinton to be more wise in dealing with racial issues? Are you surprised that the laws passed during his time are among the harshest?

~ ~ ~

question 6

The author uses the symbols of the noose, the box, and Rosa Parks. Do the symbols effectively convey black discrimination? In what way?

~~~

question 7

The motif of closure and mazes is used in the book to portray the difficult process of getting justice done through the legal system. How does going through a maze make you feel? Is the maze symbol appropriate in conveying discrimination?

~~~

~ ~ ~

question 8

The image of the ghetto is used in the book to highlight discrimination in black neighborhoods. Young men are presumed criminals by the police even if the did no crimes. Do you get a clear picture of the ghetto as described by the author? What words of description come to mind?

~ ~ ~

~~~

question 9

Alexander opens the book with a personal revelation of how she perceived racial discrimination before she came to the conclusion of the new Jim Crow. How do you describe your beliefs about racial discrimination before and after reading the book? Does the book open your eyes to new truths?

~~~

~~~

question 10

Alexander is concerned that Americans, including blacks, are looking the other way when it comes to mass incarceration of black men. She says the War on Drugs in the 80s caused the breakdown of inner-city communities. How do you feel about the lack of concern from civil rights activists about mass incarceration? Is there anything you can do about it?

~~~

~~~

question 11

Inmates released from jail and reentering society are not given a fair chance of establishing a new life. Social stigma and harsh rules about not being able to own homes and voting rights prevent them from integration. How do you feel about this? Do you think there should more compassion on people who spent time in jail and who willingness to reform?

~~~

~ ~ ~

question 12

Alexander's research reveals that majority of drug dealers and drug users are white but majority (three-fourths) who go to jail for drug offenses are blacks or Latino. What can you say about this data? Why do you think there is a discrepancy in the number of white drug offenders and non-whites who go to prison?

~ ~ ~

question 13

Incarcerated blacks who are released from prison have a hard time getting jobs. Employers almost always refuse applicants who check the box with the question about imprisonment. This adds to the marginalization of young men who are meted harsh penalties for minor crimes. How do you feel about giving jobs to people who spent time in prison? Should they be given the chance to work?

~ ~ ~

~ ~ ~

question 14

The New Jim Crow was first published in 2010 and is considered the secular bible by social activists. The book is used in their consciousness raising activities in schools, colleges, churches, community centers and prisons. Do you think many people have become aware of mass incarceration since the book was published? Are you aware of anything that has been done to correct the situation?

~ ~ ~

~~~

question 15

Alexander uses vigorous and persuasive language. She also has the ability to make abstract concepts understandable. Can you cite examples of her vigorous language? How does this affect the message of the book?

~~~

question 16

Forbes review says the book gives an account of how a legal system replaced the old Jim Crow . It "keeps the majority of minorities in a permanent state of disenfranchisement." Do you think many minorities are disenfranchised? Does the legal system keep them that way?

~ ~ ~

~ ~ ~

question 17

Publishers Weekly review says the book offers an acute analysis of mass incarceration and its effects It is provocative in revealing that colorblindness and affirmative action can confuse the vision of justice. Have you reconsidered your understanding of justice, colorblindness, and affirmative action after reading the book?

~ ~ ~

~ ~ ~

question 18

The New Jim Crow stayed in *The New York Times* bestseller list for over a year. Why do you think it stayed a bestseller for a long time?

~ ~ ~

question 19

According to David Levering Lewis, Pulitzer Prize winner and history professor, reading the book leads to a "terrible realization." He likens the American criminal justice system to the gulag of the Soviet Union. Do you think this is an appropriate comparison? Did you have a terrible realization after reading the book?

~ ~ ~

~ ~ ~

question 20

The Daily Kos review says the book guides readers through the labyrinth that is the American justice system. Do you agree that the system is like a labyrinth? Can you cite examples of the labyrinth-like justice system?

~ ~ ~

Introducing the Author

When Barack Obama was elected President of the United States, *The New Jim Crow* author Michelle Alexander was elated. She felt hopeful for the future of her three children who just witnessed that an African American can become president of America. Her elation however was tempered by the awareness of the new Jim Crow which is unjustly putting black men behind bars and socially marginalizing them for life. The night of the election night party, she came out of the party venue and saw a black man handcuffed and on his knees by the gutter while the police stood next to him, talking and ignoring him. She wondered what the Obama victory meant for him.

She wrote the book as a result of the realization that a caste-like system exists and made possible through the criminal justice system, marginalizing blacks who are victims of mass incarceration. Her work for the American Civil Liberties Union (ACLU) made her see the racial bias being implemented in the system, a bias that reminded her of racism legally implemented through the Jim Crow laws in the past century. Before her realization of the existence of a caste system, she admits that she once fully believed that racism in the US is part of America's past, not of the present.

Alexander became a civil rights lawyer after being inspired by the civil rights movement in the 1950s and 1960s. She used to believe that the Jim Crow policies belong to the past and though there is still much to be done to gain full multiracial democracy, there is real progress in the lives of African Americans. She thought her job as a civil rights lawyer was to defend affirmative action against attacks. She thought crime in black neighborhoods were a result of poverty and lack of access to education. Her beliefs were proven wrong as she eventually saw that a caste system was in operation though invisible to people like her who worked fighting against injustices.

Alexander's book was made possible through the 2005 Soros Courtesy of Zocalo Public Square Justice Fellowship. She teaches in universities and works with academic institutes that do research on race, ethnicity, and civil rights. The book is awarded best in nonfiction by the NAACP in March 2011.

Previous to teaching in universities, Alexander was director of an ACLU project which focused on equity in education and the reform of the criminal justice system. It was with her work with the project that exposed her to racial bias implemented by the law. Following her realization, she launched and led the DWB Campaign which fought against profiling of suspected criminals based on race.

Alexander took up law at Stanford University She worked for the US Supreme Court and the Court of Appeals after law school. She now spends much of her time doing freelance writing, public speaking and working with organizations advocating for the end of mass incarceration. Her most important preoccupation however is raising her three children a job she considers the most challenging and rewarding.

Fireside Questions

"What would you do?"

Tip: These questions can be a fun exercise as it spurs creativity among the readers by allowing alternate scene endings and "if this was you" questions.

~~~

question 21

When Barack Obama was elected President of the United States, Michelle Alexander felt hopeful for the future of her three children. Why do you think Obama's win gave her hope for her children?

~~~

question 22

The night of the election night party, Alexander saw a black man handcuffed by the police and on his knees by the gutter. She wondered what the Obama victory meant for the handcuffed man. What came to your mind as you read her account of Obama's win and the black man's arrest? Does this in incident evoke any strong feelings from you?

~ ~ ~

question 23

Her work with the American Civil Liberties Union (ACLU) made her see the racial bias being implemented in the criminal justice system. It reminded her of the racial discrimination in the past implemented through Jim Crow laws. Why do you think racial discrimination continues in present-day America? Why did the change in American laws not eradicate discrimination?

~~~

question 24

She thought it is not discrimination that made black people's lives difficult. Poverty and lack of access to education resulted to criminals, she thought. But her beliefs were proven wrong as she eventually saw a caste system in operation. Why is racial discrimination, not poverty and lack of education, that is the real reason behind the marginalization of blacks?

question 25

She also thought that her job as a civil rights lawyer was to defend affirmative action against those who oppose it. Why do you think affirmative action is not the solution to the racial problem as she once thought?

question 26

Alexander is a civil rights lawyer who worked with ACLU before she discovered the caste-like system being created by mass incarceration of blacks. If she worked with another organization instead of ACLU, do you think she would have discovered the truth of the new Jim Crow? Would she have eventually known about it as a civil rights lawyer working outside ACLU?

~ ~ ~

question 27

Despite Obama's election as president, mass incarceration proved that black progress is still far from complete. If Obama did not win the presidency, how would have this affected the fight against mass incarceration led by Alexander? Do you think it would have been harder for Alexander to campaign against mass incarceration and discrimination in the legal system?

~ ~ ~

question 28

Aside from her advocacy against mass incarceration, Alexander is preoccupied with taking care of her three children, a job she considers most challenging and rewarding. If she does not have children, do you think she would be as passionate about working for black rights and multiracial democracy? Do you think her passion for her work is related to the future of her children?

~ ~ ~

question 29

Alexander became a civil rights lawyer after being inspired by the civil rights movement. If she chose not to become a lawyer, would she have continued to fight for black rights? Would her racial background be enough inspiration for her to fight against discrimination even if she chose not to become a lawyer?

~~~

question 30

Alexander says many African Americans do not believe discrimination is happening through mass incarceration. They choose to look the other way. If the rest of the black population are to join the protest against the new Jim Crow, what do you think would happen?

~~~

Quiz Questions

"Ready to Announce the Winners?"

Tip: Create a leaderboard and track scores to see who gets the most correct answers. Winners required. Prizes optional.

quiz question 1

Her work with the _____ opened Alexander's eyes to the reality that the criminal justice system discriminates against blacks.

~~~

quiz question 2

When _____ was elected President of the United States, Alexander felt elated. Her children just witnessed an African American become president of America.

~~~

~ ~ ~

quiz question 3

In the _____ chapter of the book, Alexander tells the history of race and racial relations including the Civil War, the Reconstruction, the Jim Crow laws, and the Civil Rights Movement.

~ ~ ~

~ ~ ~

quiz question 4

True or False: The New Jim Crow was first published in 2012 and was on the New York Times bestseller list for over a year.

~ ~ ~

~~~

quiz question 5

True or False: Alexander discovered that most of drug dealers and users are white but three-fourths who go to jail for drug offenses are blacks or Latino.

~~~

~~~

quiz question 6

True or False: Closures and mazes are used in the book to portray the difficult process of achieving justice through the legal system.

~~~

quiz question 7

True or False: Alexander reveals that young black men are meted harsh penalties for minor crimes. After imprisonment, they have a hard time getting obs. Job application requires them to check the box that tells they have been imprisoned. This adds to their marginalization.

~~~

quiz question 8

The _____ in the 1950s and 1960s inspired
Alexander to become a civil rights lawyer.

~~~

~ ~ ~

quiz question 9

The New Jim Crow won the NAACP Image Award for best _____ in March 2011.

~ ~ ~

~~~

quiz question 10

True or False: Alexander's beliefs about justice and the criminal legal system were proven wrong when she saw that a caste system was actually in operation.

~~~

quiz question 11

True or False: Her most important job is raising her three children. It is the most challenging and rewarding job.

~ ~ ~

quiz question 12

True or False: Following her realization of racial bias in the criminal justice system, she launched and led the "Drinking While Black or Brown Campaign" or DWB Campaign.

~~~

Quiz Answers

1. ACLU
2. Barack Obama
3. First
4. False
5. True
6. True
7. True
8. civil rights movement
9. nonfiction
10. True
11. True
12. False

Ways to Continue Your Reading

EVERY month, our team runs through a wide selection of books to pick the best titles fo readers and reading groups, and promote these titles to our thousands of readers sometimes with free downloads, sale dates, and additional brochures.

If you have not yet read the original work or would like to read it again, get the book here.

Want to register yourself or a book group? It's free and takes 1-click.

Register here.

On the Next Page...

Please write us your reviews! Any length would be fine but we'd appreciate hearing you more! We'd be SO grateful.

Till next time,

BookHabits

"Loving Books is Actually a Habit"